Mystic Shells
Shell Art by Oceanmuse

Rita McDonald

Copyright © 2018 Rita S. McDonald

All rights reserved.

ISBN:1986879178
ISBN-13:9781986879170

DEDICATION

To my Mother, Rosemary Newell Gibson, who believed in me and allowed me to follow my heart.

CONTENTS

	Acknowledgments	i
1	Shamans & Ancient Warriors	1
2	Mermaids & Mermen	Pg 7
3	The Blue Period	Pg 13
4	Mantras	Pg 17
5	Art Deco	Pg 20
6	Addendum	Pg 23

ACKNOWLEDGMENTS

I'd like to acknowledge the Art History Department at the University of Oklahoma which gave me my degree and the courage to express my own art.

SHAMANS AND ANCIENT WARRIORS

Experience the touch of a majestic almost spiritual and other-worldly portrayal reflected in these pieces.

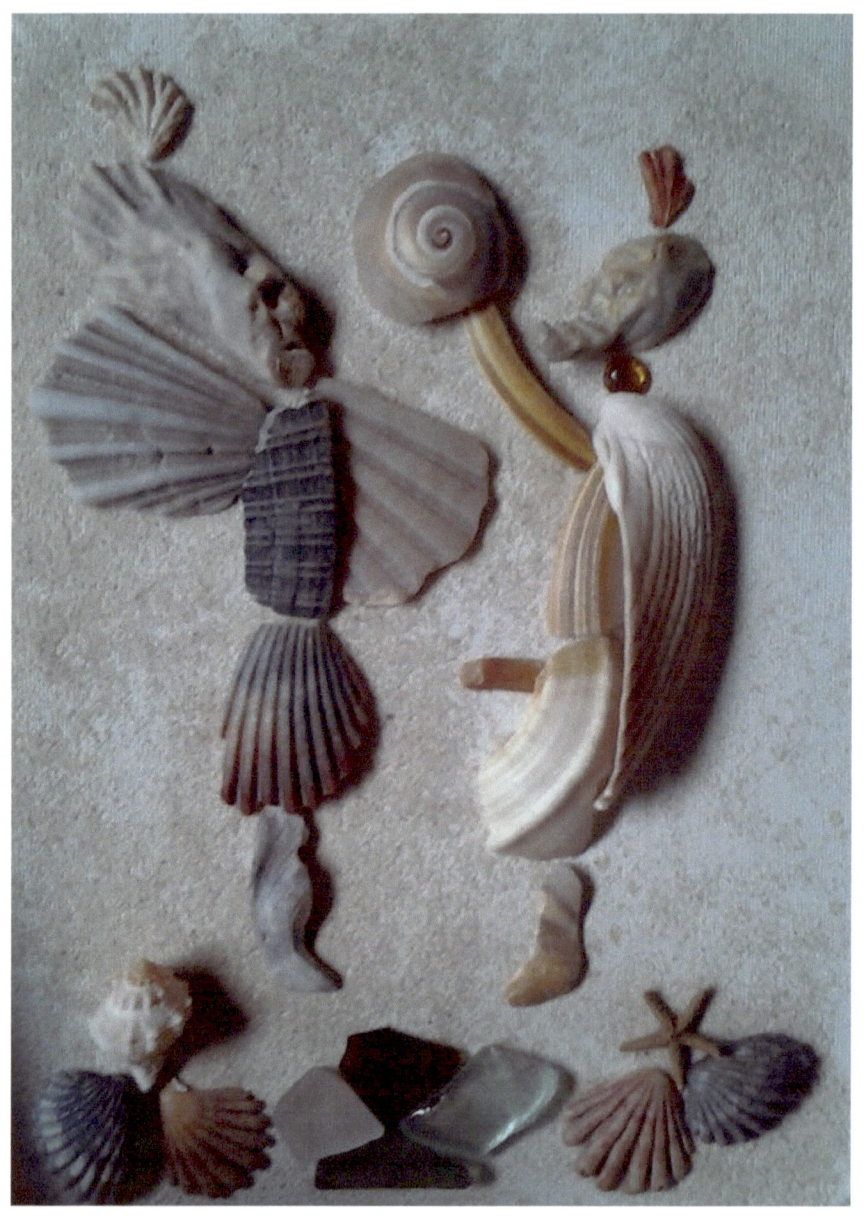

Mystic Shells-Shell Art By Oceanmuse

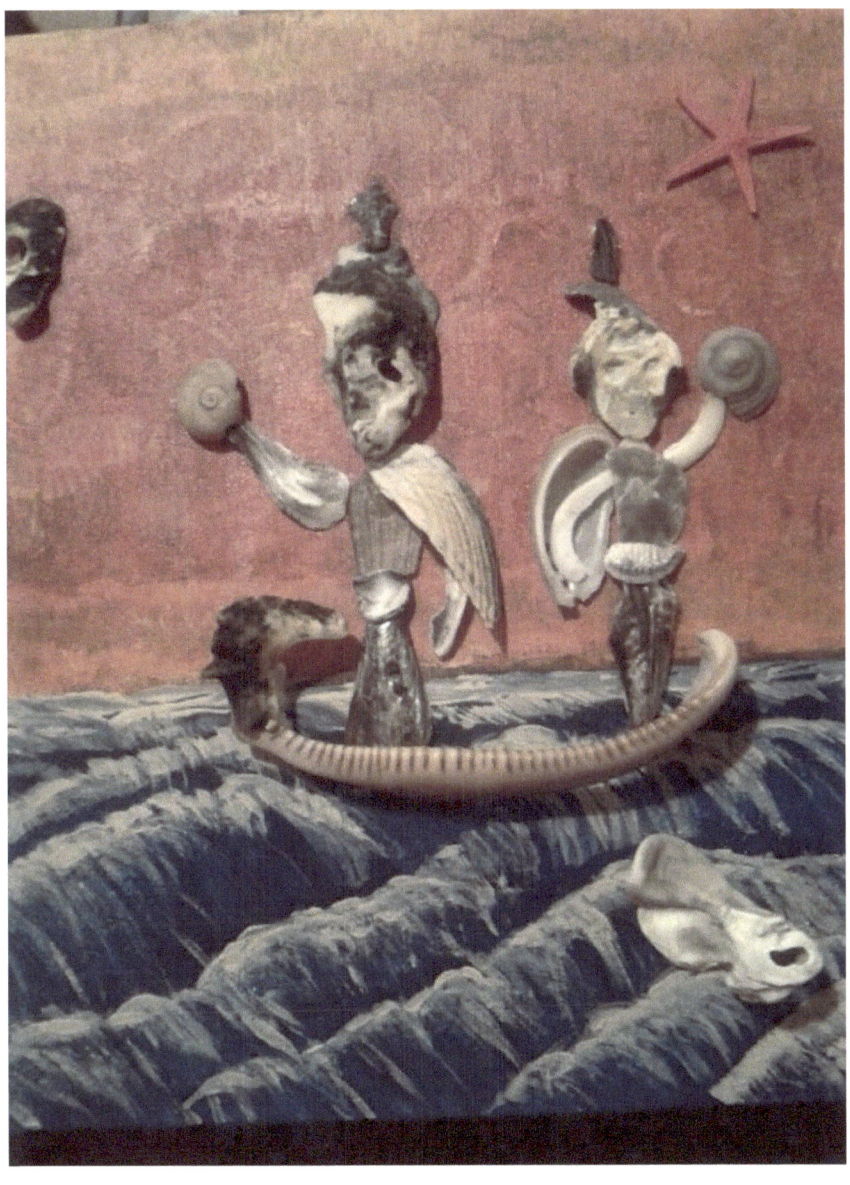

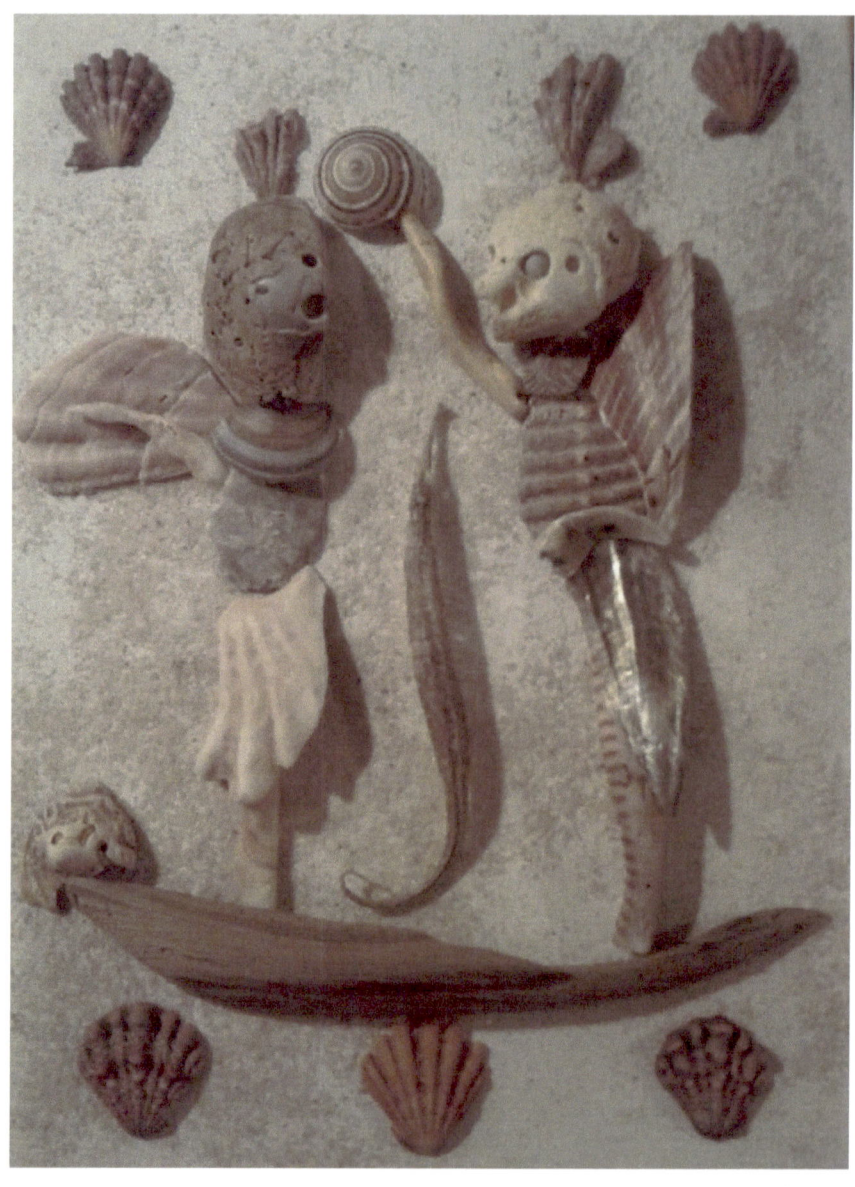

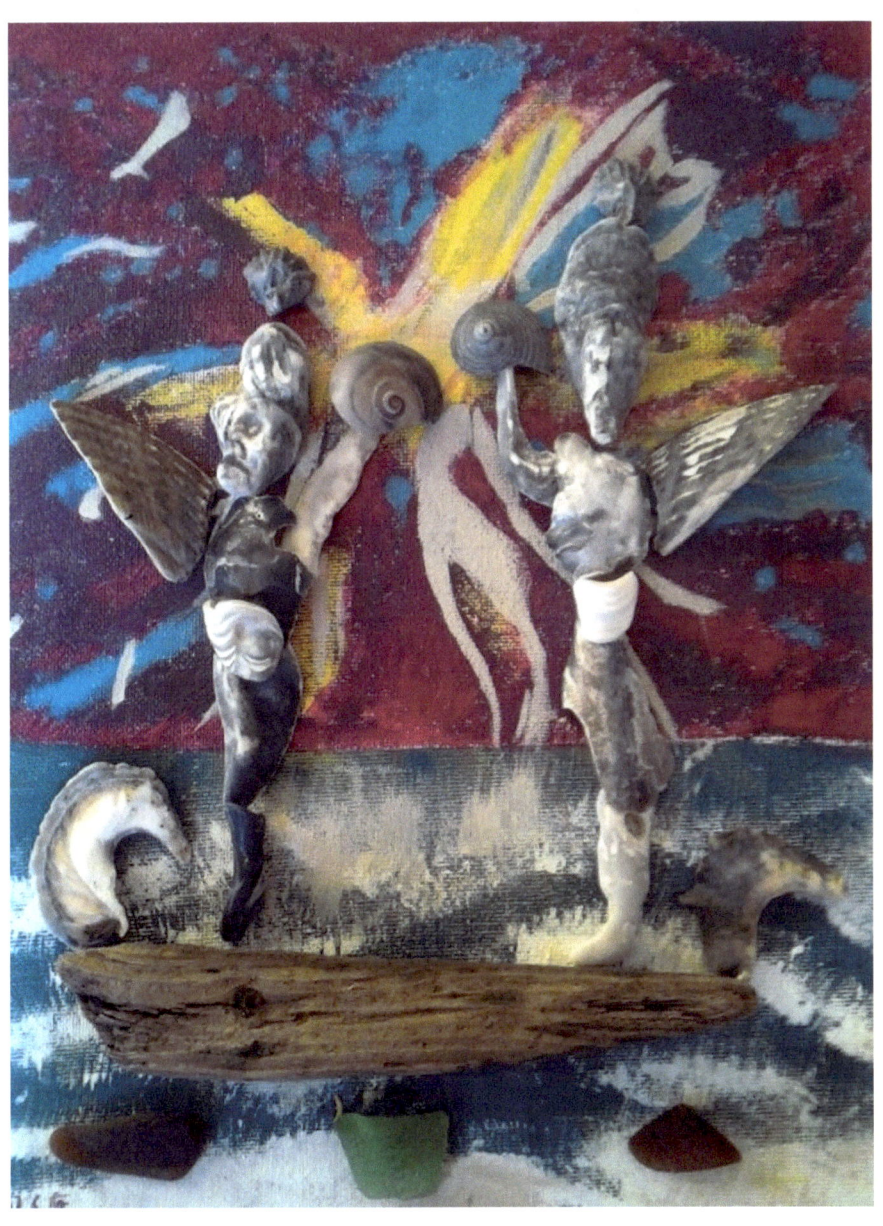

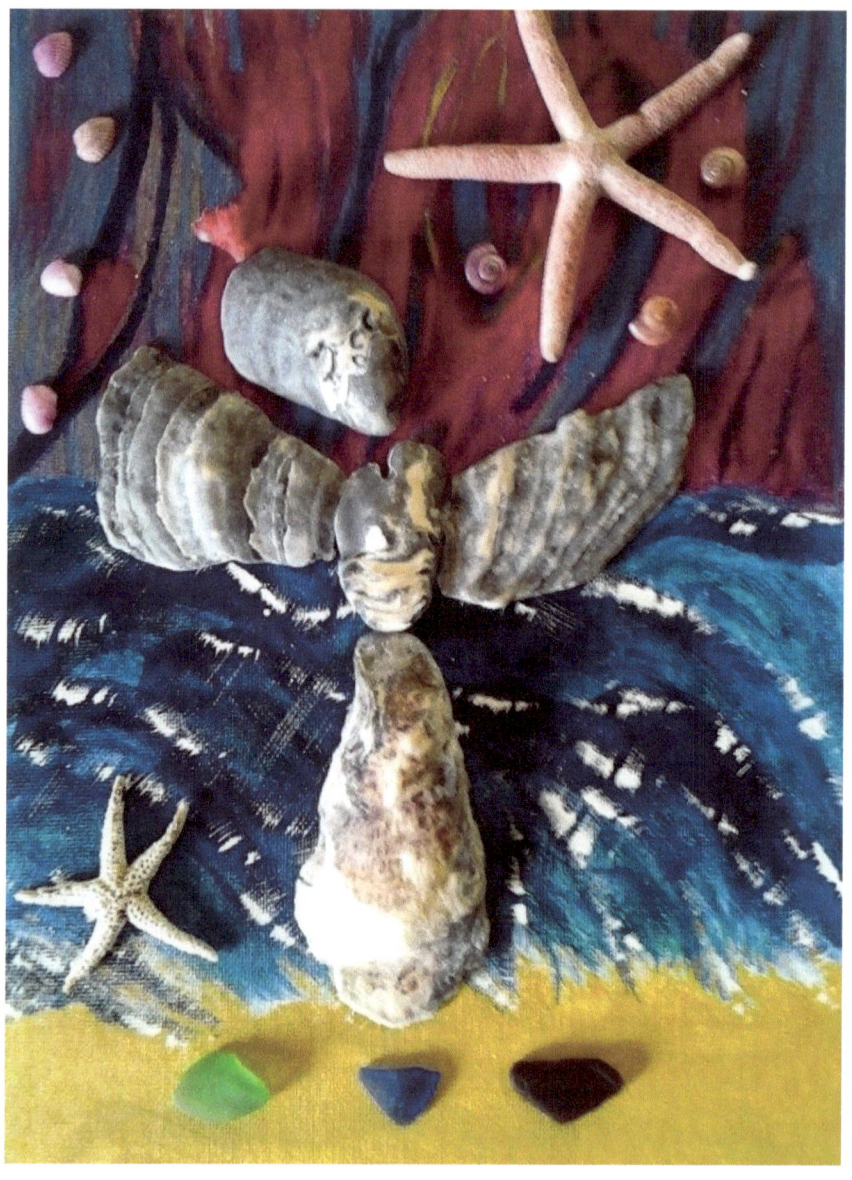

MERMAIDS AND MERMEN

Rita McDonald

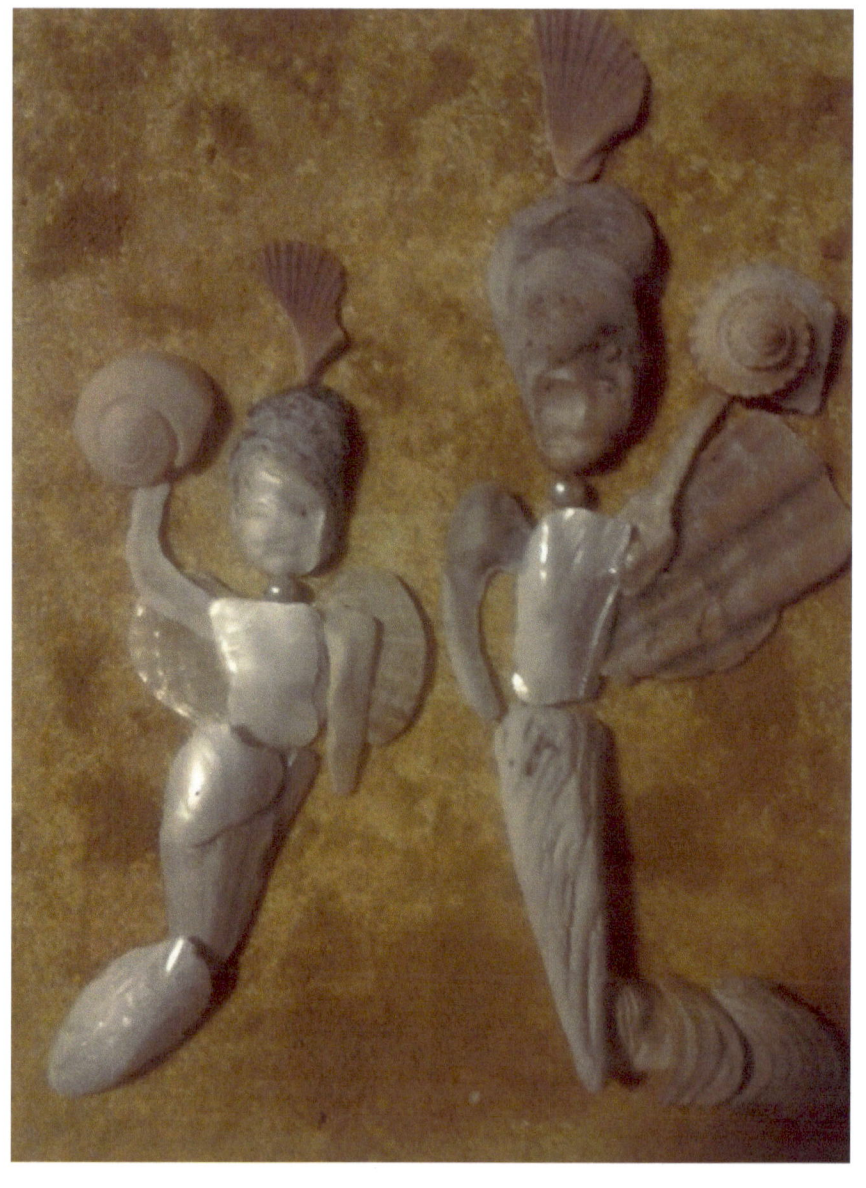

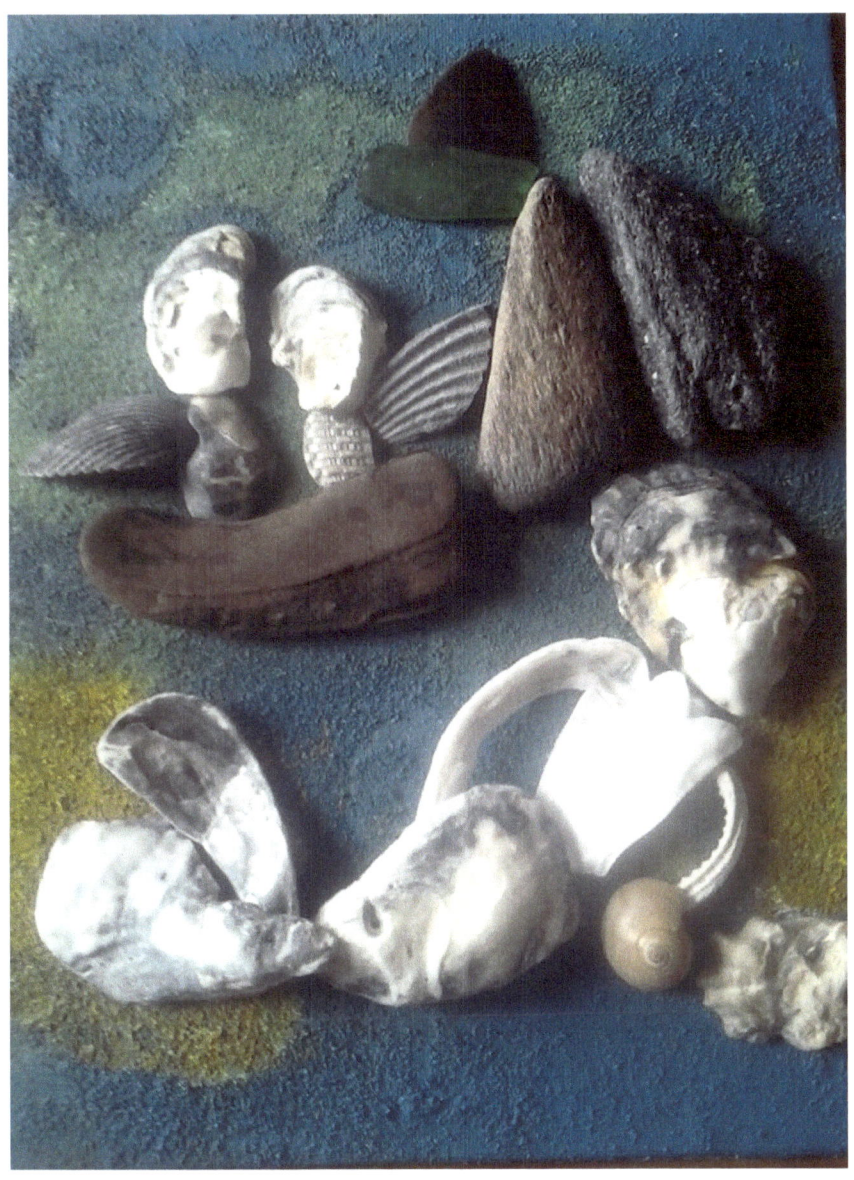

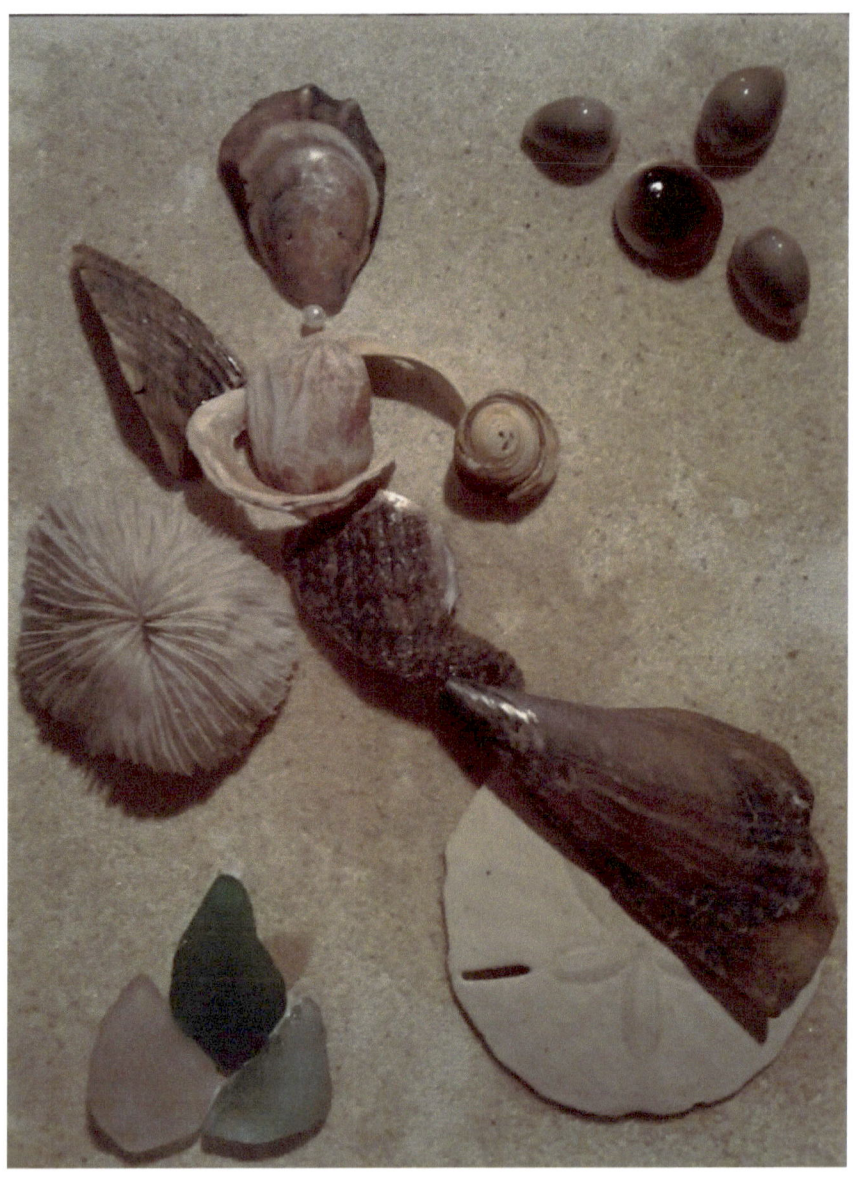

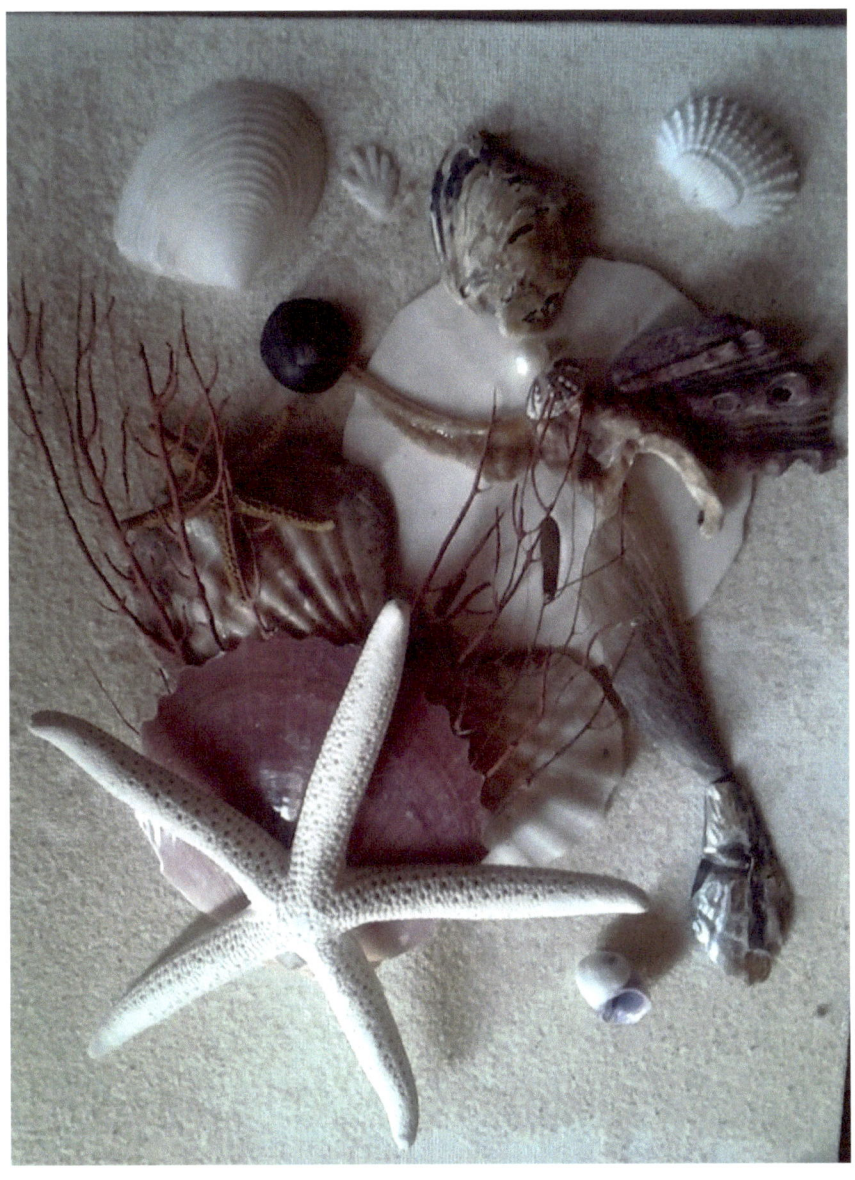

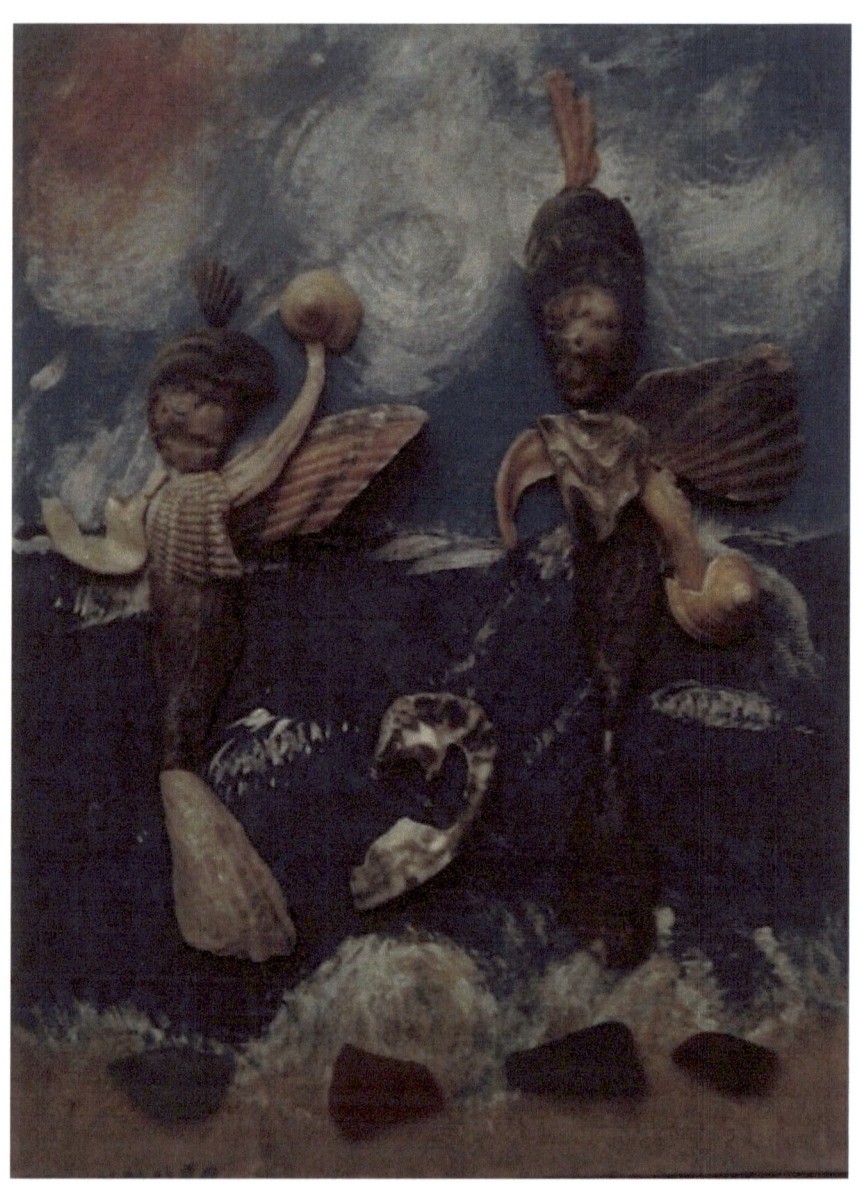

THE BLUE PERIOD

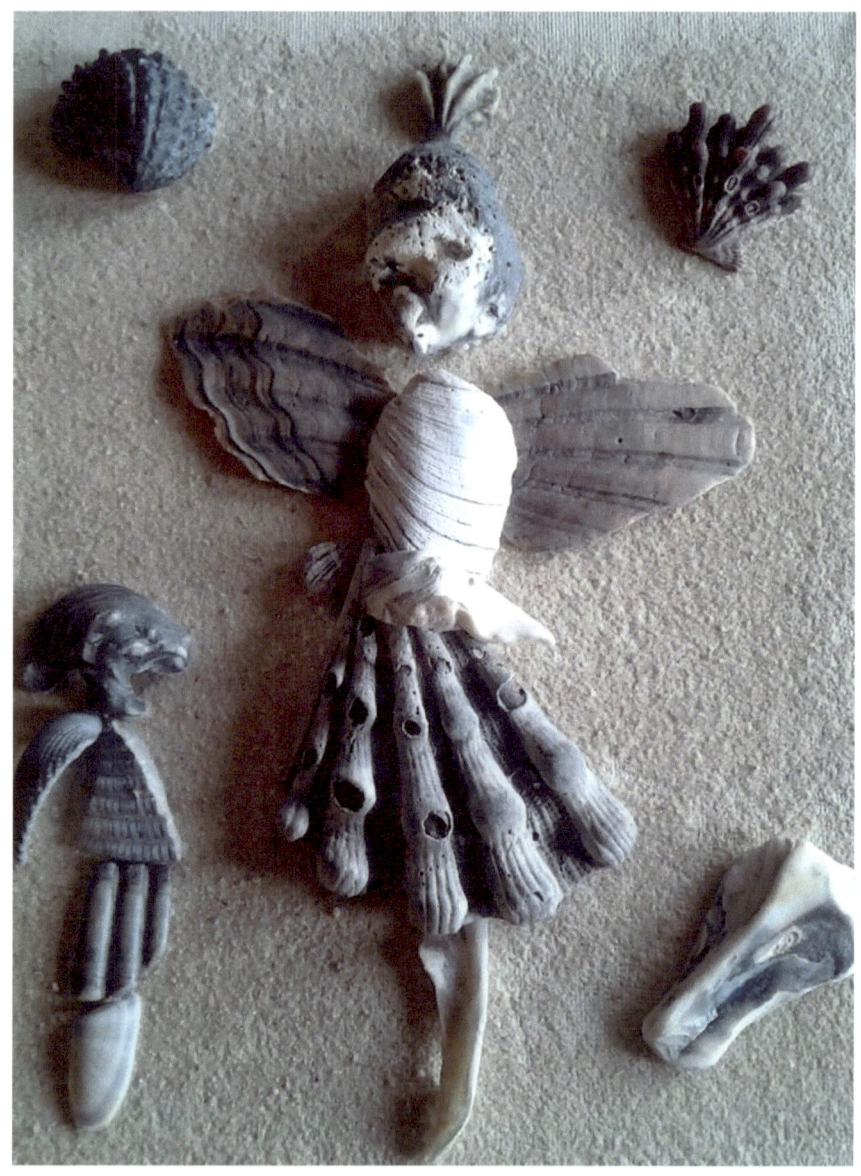

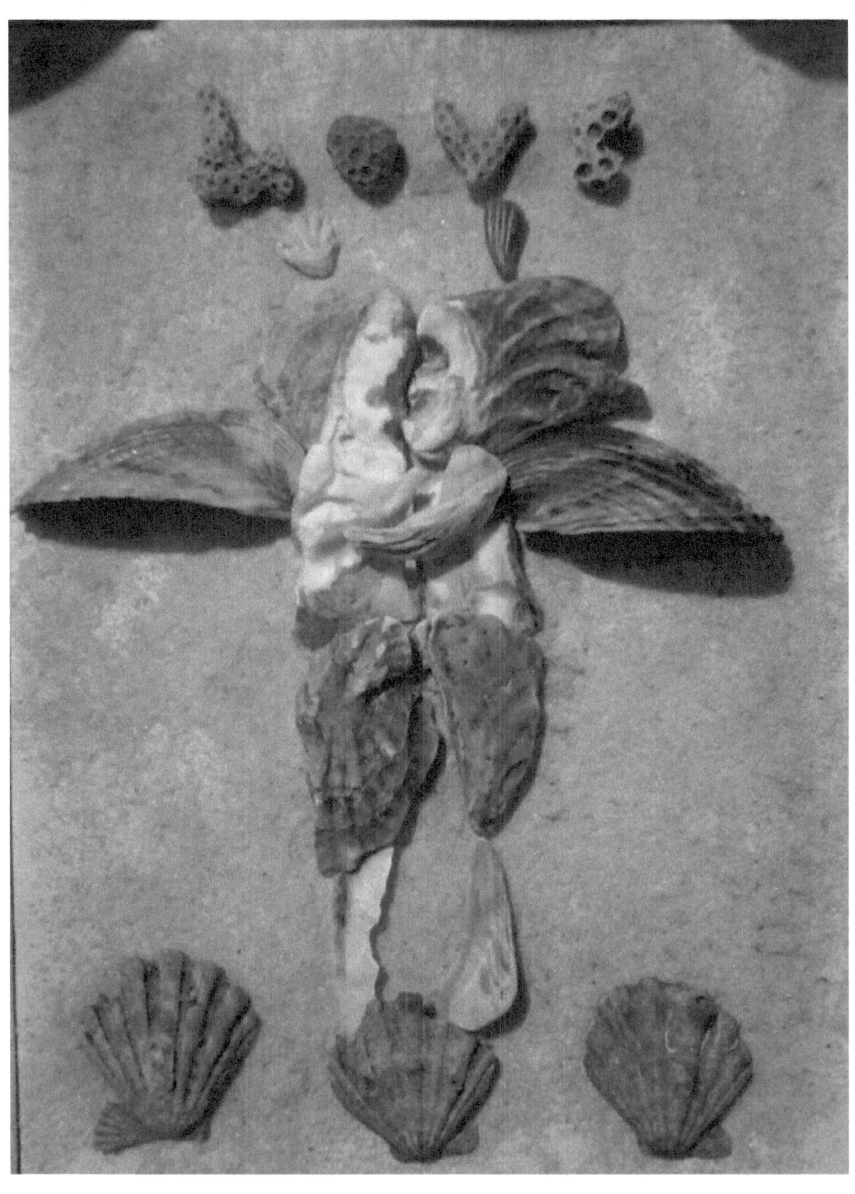

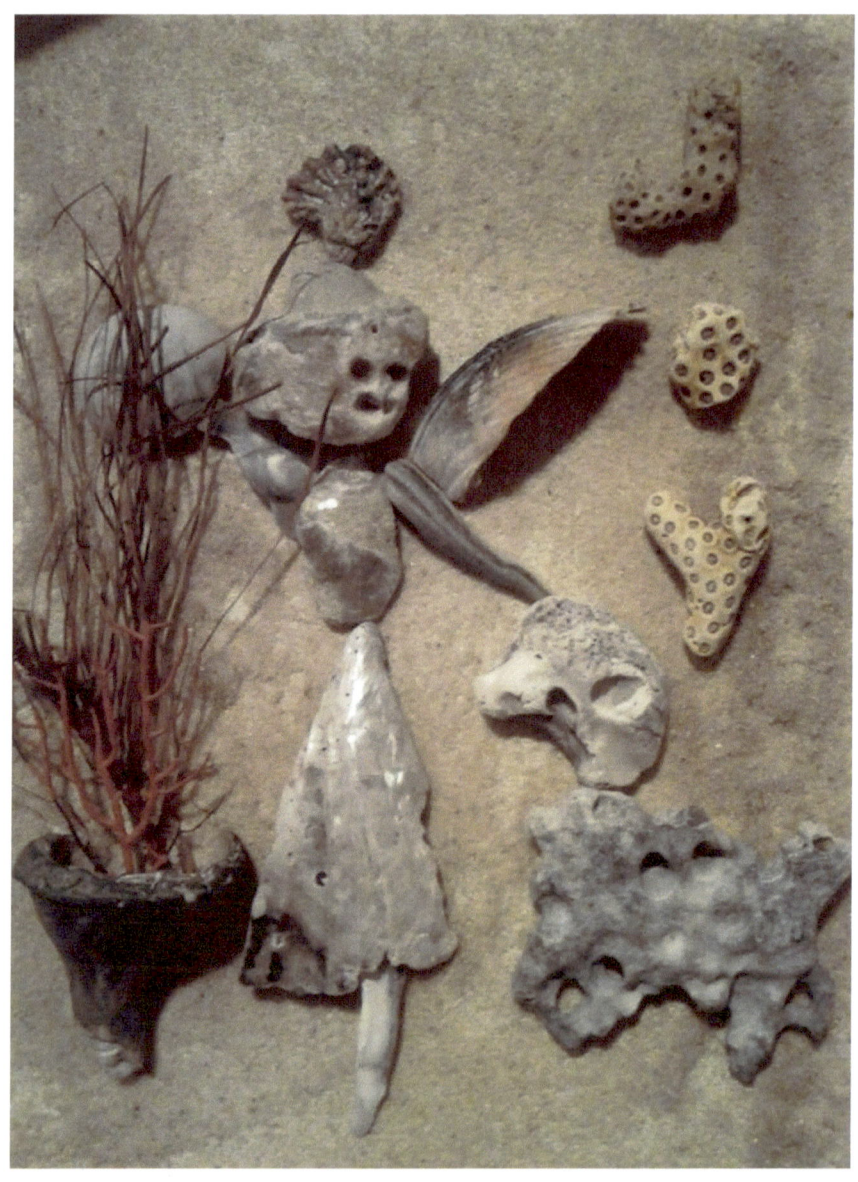

MANTRAS

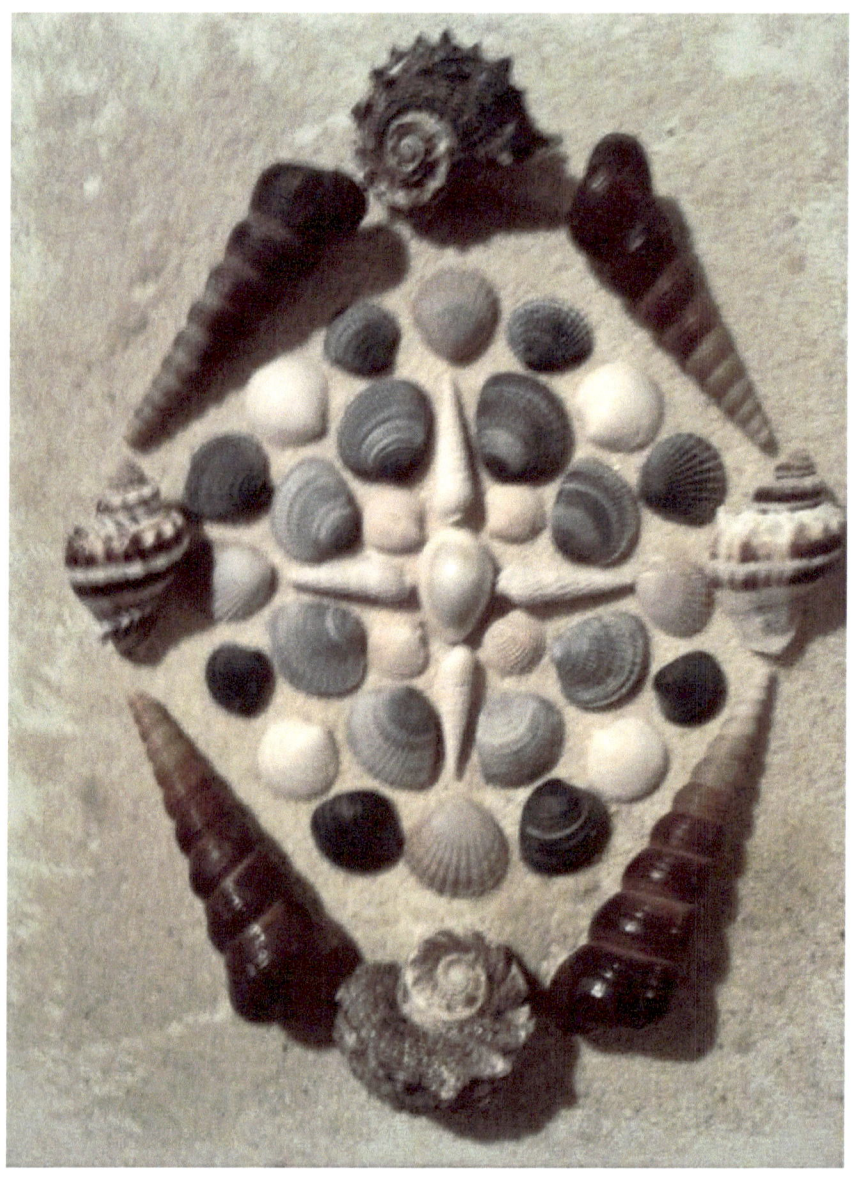

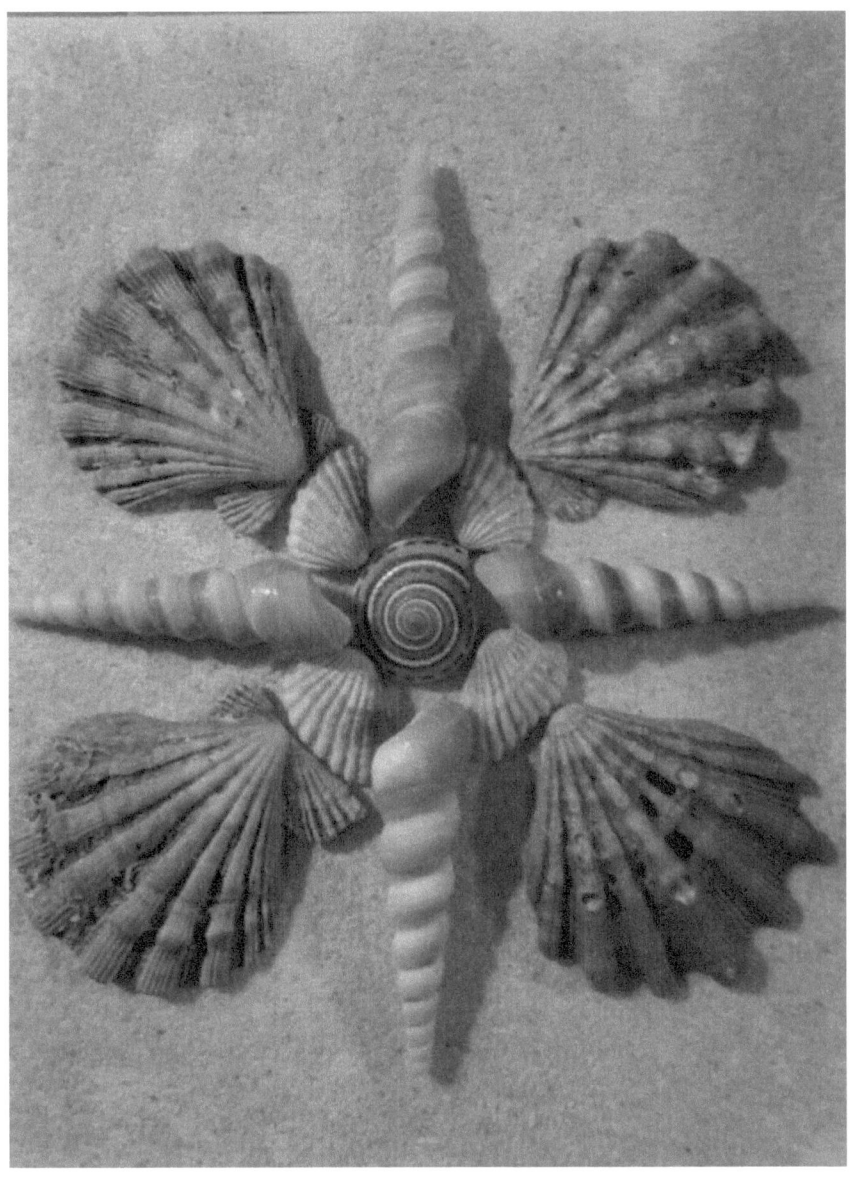

ART DECO

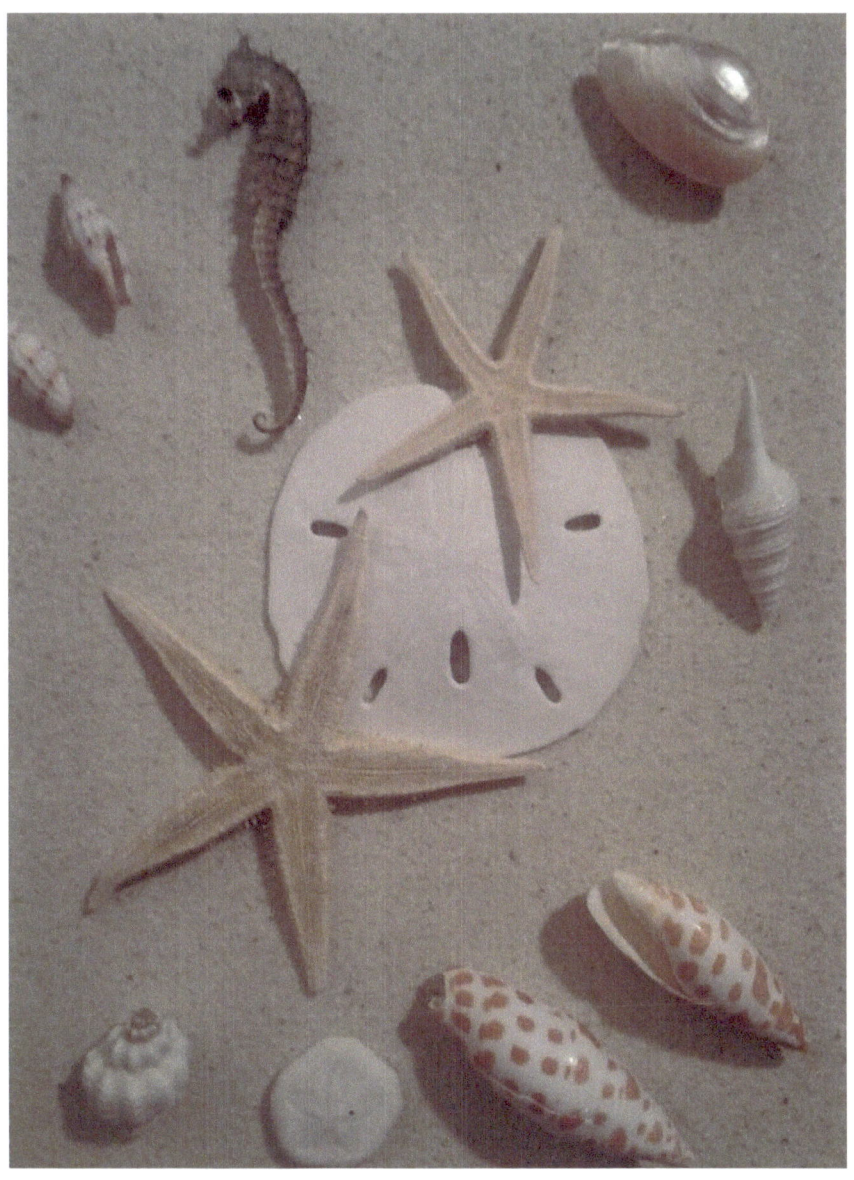

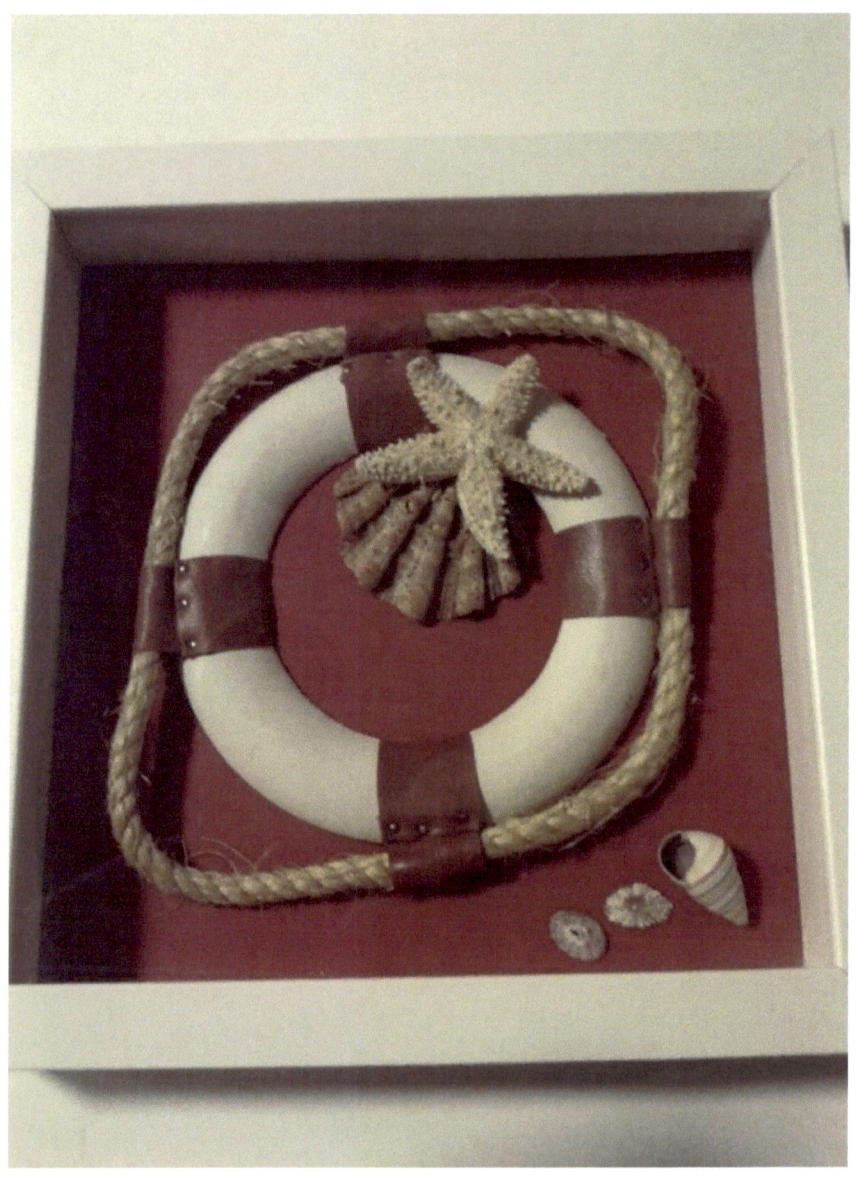

ADDENDUM

Hi guys and gals, I hope you enjoyed my art, if so, there is much more to see on my website artbythesea@wix.com/oceanmuse like the names of the artwork and prices and much more art. If you'd like to contact me, send me an email at inspirationsbythesea@gmail.com or search for me on Google.

Thanks for purchasing this book and allowing me to share my art with you .

ABOUT THE AUTHOR

The artist resides near North Topsail Beach, North Carolina where she moved to get over the loss of her husband. She was inspired by the many faces she found in the seashells and soon began her art. Her works are on display at the Mermaids Purse in Surf City NC and Studio 1515 in Wilmington, NC

www.ingramcontent.com/pod-product-compliance
Lightning Source LLC
Chambersburg PA
CBHW040300220526
45473CB00002B/540